Encounter Grace

MOMENTS
HOPE, JOY, *and* PEACE

BECKY ELDREDGE
Author of *Busy Lives & Restless Souls* and *The Inner Chapel*

LOYOLA PRESS.
A JESUIT MINISTRY

LOYOLA PRESS.
A JESUIT MINISTRY
www.loyolapress.com

Cover art credit: polygraphus/iStock/Getty Images, Lilett/iStock/Getty Images, Shutterstock/GoodStudio
Author photo: Camille Delaune

ISBN: 978-0-8294-6060-5
Library of Congress Control Number: 2025942835

Published in Chicago, IL
Printed in the United States of America
25 26 27 28 29 30 31 31 32 33 Versa 10 9 8 7 6 5 4 3 2 1

And remember,

I am with you always,

to the end of the age.

—Matthew 28:20

A Note to Readers

Dear Friend,

I invite you to join me in exploring the beautiful gift of the inner chapel, where God resides within each of us. This sacred space is where we come to understand our longing for God and recognize God's deep longing to be in relationship with us.

In this small book, you'll find brief passages and questions for reflection, prayer, and journaling, each designed to help you connect with God in your everyday life. Whether you're sipping your morning coffee, winding down before bed, or finding a quiet moment amid your busy day, this book is here to support you in embracing the gift of your inner chapel.

When we can embrace the gift of our inner chapel, we discover an ever-present source of hope, joy, and peace that comes from a profound connection with God.

Peace,

Becky

An Invitation to Deeper Waters

I can imagine Jesus standing with us on the beach, pointing into the ocean of endless possibilities of our relationship with God and asking us, "Are you ready to go into the waters? Do you want to go deeper?" Even though Jesus is right there with us, pointing the way, it is also as if the ocean of spiritual possibility beckons us to enter, awakening in us that same desire to put out into the deep as the ocean does my kids when they swim. It reminds me of the line in the Psalms, "Deep calls to deep" (Psalm 42:7). This beckoning and searching we feel is the Holy Spirit inviting us and drawing us ever deeper into our relationship with God. This deep-down desire is just one of many indications that God longs for us.

What does it mean to put out into the deep when it comes to your spiritual life?

What might it mean for you personally to accept this invitation?

Always Accompanied

There are two important things for us to remember about this invitation from Jesus to enter the waters of faith. First, he never leaves our side. We are always accompanied by him. Second, he is always inviting us to go deeper, eventually drawing us into water where we can no longer touch the bottom, and we are invited to even go under and swim in the quiet waters below the surface. No matter where we are in our faith journey, there is more to learn and explore in our relationship with God.

When are you most aware of Jesus being at your side?

How might Jesus be drawing you into the deeper waters of faith?

The Unending Hunger

During college, I would attend a retreat or event that filled my tank and fueled my hunger for God even more. I would return home, and days later the crash would hit, and I found myself lost, aimless, and searching again. There was a hunger in me that felt as if it could never be satisfied, despite my efforts to grow my relationship with God through continued attendance at various programs. Maybe you feel like this now or have felt it in the past.

Reflect on a time when you felt fired up because of a spiritual event, only to lose your enthusiasm soon afterward. What hunger did you feel then, and are you experiencing a similar hunger now?

How might God be speaking to you in this?

Finding Strength Within

The greatest comfort and hope of my life is this gift of the inner chapel. Without it, I would be lost and still searching like crazy for the next thing to bring me a spiritual high or the next thing to satisfy my longing. My strength is within. It's not my willpower or my personal drive or gumption, but someone: God within me, who is readily available at any given moment. Here, in my inner chapel, I meet God and experience the promises that come with this ever-deepening relationship.

Why is our inner chapel such a comfort and source of hope?

What does it mean to you to know that your inner strength comes not from a personal attribute or an aspect of your personality but rather from God?

The Inner Chapel

The gift of the inner chapel is within each one of us. It is a place where we can come to understand not only our longing for God but also God's longing to be in relationship with us. We each have an inner chapel, a space within us where God resides. This means that at any point in our day we have a sacred space where we can pause for prayer. It is a space to which only you and God have access. This means we can call on God at any moment, no matter what we are doing. It is where we meet God, get to know Jesus, and learn the ways the Holy Spirit works in our lives.

When, where, and how do you typically enter, or access, your inner chapel?

When have you sensed God's longing to be in relationship with you?

The Legacy of Faith

The legacy of men and women leaning on the strength of their inner chapels to grow in relationship with God continues from Jesus to the apostles and the early church, to the long array of saints who went before us. They leave us glimpses of their wisdom about how to access and draw on the resources of the inner chapel. We learn from St. Catherine of Siena's image of the inner cell, St. Teresa of Ávila's wisdom in the interior castle, and St. Thérèse of Lisieux sharing how "Jesus teaches me in secret" and how "the Kingdom of God is within me at each moment."

Can you name someone you either know about or know personally who consistently draws strength from their inner chapel?

What might you learn from them about tapping into your inner chapel?

Hope in God's Promises

I believe there is a need more than ever to invite people to embrace the inner chapel and encourage people to grow an intimate relationship with God. Rather than forget the promises of God, our world needs to cling to them as never before. The good news is not only that the promises of God exist but also that we can go to our inner chapels every day, despite our own busyness and the world's chaos, and meet God within us.

In what ways do you cling to the promises of God? What experiences are most likely to draw you into your inner chapel?

What changes can you make in your daily life that will facilitate a close relationship with God?

A Recipe for Prayer

Learning how to pray can feel much like learning how to make crawfish étouffée. There is not one secret recipe. You learn a few foundational basics, and then you learn to taste, tweak, and season based on where God has you on your faith journey.

How has your recipe for prayer changed over the course of your life?

What has remained constant?

The Trinity of Prayer

In Louisiana cooking, many dishes, such as crawfish étouffée, begin with the "trinity"—onion, celery, and bell pepper. From these three ingredients, a wide array of Cajun dishes is made: gumbo, jambalaya, crawfish étouffée, red beans and rice, and shrimp creole, among many others. In our prayer lives, there is a "trinity" that is essential as well: our time of prayer, our place of prayer, and our space of prayer. If we want to access the resources of the inner chapel, we need to lean into an intentional prayer time.

Do you lean into an intentional prayer time? Reflect on your trinity of prayer essentials.

What is your time for prayer?

Where is your place of prayer? How do you create a personal space for prayer?

Different Paths

There is an expansive list of prayer methods that we can bring into our foundational prayer time. Each is distinctive and offers a special way of relating to God. Part of our work of going to our inner chapel every day is discerning which prayer method God is inviting us to use.

What have been your favorite prayer methods over the course of your life of prayer? How do these methods help you relate to God?

Do they still work well for you now?

Awareness

Once in your prayer place, intentionally place yourself in the presence of God. Take a few deep breaths. As you breathe in and out slowly, remind yourself that you are never alone, and that God is with you right now.

What do you do to transition into your prayer experience?

What helps you become more aware of God's presence? What interferes with your ability to connect with God?

Seeking Grace

St. Ignatius invites us to name the grace we seek at the start of every prayer period. After placing yourself in the presence of God, simply go to God with the question, *What is the grace I seek?* Notice what word arises in your mind and heart. Are you seeking rest? Peace? Clarity? Courage? Hope? Light? Love? Mercy? And on and on the list might go. When a word arises in your thoughts, turn this into a prayer: "God, as I begin, I seek the grace of __________." Then begin your prayer time using the prayer method God is inviting you to use at the moment.

Ask yourself: What is the grace I am seeking at this moment?

How can I turn a desire for a grace into a prayer?

Reflecting on Your Journey

At the end of your prayer time, St. Ignatius also invites us to do a review of prayer. This simply involves a look back over the minutes spent in prayer with the question *What happened here?* It might be helpful to purchase a journal where you can jot down what you noticed in prayer. Perhaps you write the word or phrase from Scripture that caught your heart. Maybe you jot down a memory or image that God stirred in prayer. You might note the feelings that rose within you as you prayed.

Why is it a good idea to review your prayer?

Think of the last prayer experience you had so that you can better understand what happened during that prayer time.

Awakening to Prayer

As you continue to lean into your intentional prayer time, you may also find it helpful to do a weekly review of prayer. This is similar to the daily review of prayer; to do a weekly review, you look back over your daily notes of prayer to jot down what has happened in this week's prayer time. The practice of reviewing prayer is a beautiful tool to help discern the movement of God within our hearts and also within our lives. The art of looking backward and reviewing our prayer will help us continue our forward movement and growth in God.

What is the benefit of doing a review of your prayer over a week's time?

How does looking back help you move forward?

Graceful Support

Our prayer lives often begin within a community or through some experience with others that awakens our desire for it and leaves us desiring more. It is not only about experiencing prayer but also about learning how to pray and, at some point, teaching others to pray.

Who, or what experience, awakened within you a desire to pray?

Who taught you to pray? Who was your example in praying? Have you taught others how to pray? If so, describe the experience.

The Importance of Guidance

The bottom line is this. I have never been on my own in learning how to pray. I was supported not only by God in coming to my prayer time; I also had people along the way who came alongside me and still come alongside me to teach me how to pray. As God drew me deeper into relationship, these teachers offered me tools for prayer to continue to go to my inner chapel as the seasons of my prayer life changed.

What does it mean to say that we are never on our own when it comes to learning how to pray?

What prayer tools have been offered to you during the course of your prayer life?

Growing in Prayer

Masters in any field, whether playing an instrument or practicing medicine, will say that they never stop learning. In prayer, our schooling never stops. We have to be practitioners of the very thing we are also called to teach others. Being a person of prayer means that we are not only still cooking but also still learning. We, too, even at a later stage of our spiritual lives, still need someone to come alongside us and accompany us. At the same time that we are praying and being accompanied, we are called to accompany someone else and teach them.

What was the most recent thing you learned about prayer?

Who, if anyone, accompanies you on your prayer journey? Are you ready to accompany someone else in prayer? Are you ready to be accompanied by someone in your prayer life?

The Way of Ignatian Spirituality

I believe that the Ignatian way is one that busy laypeople can find a home in today. The elements and guiding principles of Ignatian spirituality resonate and can be practiced easily within the realities of everyday life. The entire spirituality is based on learning to live as a "contemplative in action," which simply means being a person of prayer who lives out a unique call in the world. The Ignatian prayer practices give guidance on how to become a more contemplative, reflective person. Ignatian discernment wisdom offers tools to discern among the multitude of choices we face.

What is your understanding of Ignatian spirituality?

In what ways does Ignatian spirituality resonate with the realities of your everyday life?

Flexibility

The Ignatian way is not just for priests, religious brothers, or religious sisters but is a path for laypeople, too. Nor is this spirituality available only when you reach a certain stage of life and "things slow down," as I have been told more times than I can count. The Ignatian way is available to us right now as we are, where we are, no matter what stage of life we are in.

What draws you to Ignatian spirituality?

What do you hope to gain by walking the Ignatian path?

Time Management

The problem isn't that we cannot make time for God but that we often don't know how to do that. I believe we cannot delay our relationship with God to a later stage of life. From my experience of praying the Ignatian way in my own life and also listening to others' experiences from my position as an Ignatian-trained spiritual director and the twenty-plus years of facilitating Ignatian retreats, I can tell you that every one of us can make time for God with the wisdom of Ignatian spirituality to support us. We can make time for prayer.

What do you desire in your prayer life?

How do you, or how can you, make time for prayer in your busy life?

Source of Hope

I know now that the source of my hope lies within me, in the inner chapel where God resides. When I go there each day, I spend time with: someone who changed my life; someone who offers rest, love that is unconditional, and mercy that never runs out; someone who offers companionship no matter what I am facing; someone who cares enough to come after me, even when I turn away; someone who is not afraid to encourage me or even challenge me when I mess up; someone who helps me understand the unique gifts and callings of my life; someone who offers me hope, who is the source of my hope; someone who shows me that my life has meaning and that I have the capacity for joy.

In the litany above listing examples of who God is and what God does for us, which one most resonates with you?

How is God a source of hope for you?

Walking the Path

I invite you to walk this path, using the gifts of Ignatian spirituality. As we walk it, we join the millions of others who are on the larger path of Christian faith. Remember that the Ignatian way is simply one spirituality that offers us a way to get to know God. For me it has been the path that led me to understanding and experiencing the inner chapel, where I discovered the promises of God.

In addition to the Ignatian way, what other spiritualities speak to you?

What spiritual practices or experiences have helped you get to know God?

The Word

Praying with Scripture is the basis of St. Ignatius's Spiritual Exercises. Scripture plays a huge role in discovering the promises of God. As we pray with Scripture, the ancient words become ever new. In the Spiritual Exercises, we are invited to pray with Scripture and not study it. Praying with Scripture invites us to get to know who God is and the way God works. In a particular way, it helps us get to know Jesus.

What role does Scripture play in your prayer life?

Are you yearning to make fresh discoveries in Scripture of the promises of God? What steps might you take to help make this happen?

Longing for Love

St. Mother Teresa said that all human beings "long to love and be loved." We each long to be in relationship, to be known, and to know someone intimately. We long to know that we are not alone. Our human longings are what send us searching for God in the first place. Over the years, I have come to discover that my longings and the longings I notice in others simply need to be directed to God. We are longing for God, but God is also longing for us. The very things we long for, God longs to give us.

What do you find yourself longing for most at this point in your life? What does it mean to direct your longings to God?

In what ways do you sense that God is longing for you?

God in Our Restlessness

We experience God at work in our lives through the longings we feel. Sometimes it feels like restlessness. Sometimes it feels like something is off in our lives. Sometimes it is when we find ourselves searching for more and we cannot quite put our finger on what it is we are searching for. When we feel this longing, though, I want you to rest assured of something: The longing we feel is God with us. It is one of the ways God is reminding us that we are not alone, that God is with us, drawing us ever closer into relationship.

How does God work through our longings and restlessness?

When was a time that God reminded you that you were not alone?

Finding Peace

The way God calls us into relationship is by awakening in us longing or restlessness. When you notice this feeling, I invite you to wake up to the gift that you are not alone and that God is with you in that moment, longing to be in relationship with you. As St. Augustine says, "Our hearts are restless until they rest in You." Or, as Psalm 62 says, "In God alone is my soul at rest." Our restlessness is a longing for God and God longing for us. It is God's deep desire for intimacy with us, to know and be known by the beloved and share life together.

How have you experienced this sense of restlessness in your life?

What does it mean to you to rest in God? How do you describe the feeling of longing within you?

Seeking Fulfillment

When we try to satiate this restlessness with someone or something other than God, our longing will never be satisfied. Our deepest human desires to be known fully and to know someone intimately lead us into relationship with God.

Being honest with yourself, what are some of the ways you seek to satiate the restlessness in your life?

How can you bring this feeling of restlessness to God?

Designed for Eternity

The first three lines of the Principle and Foundation of the Spiritual Exercises clearly state that the goal of our life is "to live with God forever." What's beautiful about naming this as our goal is also remembering that we are designed to desire this goal. God made us in such a way that we cannot help but seek our goal, which is to live with God forever. Living with God forever does not mean in some far-off time; forever means both now and in our walk to eternal life.

What does it mean to you to know that you were designed to desire the goal of life as defined by St. Ignatius?

How can this certainty that you are meant to live with God forever help when you are tempted to seek other strategies for satisfying your restlessness?

Awakening

When we find ourselves longing for more, searching and seeking, it is often God awakening us to God's longing for a relationship with us. As the next line of the First Principle and Foundation states, "God, who loves us, gave us life." So, the one we long for loves us and created us—and the one who longs for us loves us and created us. The gnawing sensation we feel might be God getting our attention about spending time with God.

When have you experienced the gnawing sensation that God is trying to get your attention? Describe what it feels like to be awakened to God longing for a relationship with you.

What would help you grow in awareness of the longings of your heart?

Filling the Void

The something missing in our lives is often not a what but a who. The search for more is not a new item on our task list or an added responsibility but a relationship with God. The Holy Spirit moves within us and raises desires in our hearts to fulfill those longings for a relationship that fills all things, that offers unconditional love, and that provides meaning to our lives.

What difference does it make to fill whatever is missing in our lives with someone rather than something?

In practical terms, what does it mean to have a relationship with God?

Responding with Love

What, then, is our response when we feel this type of restlessness or longing? We can turn to the third line of the First Principle and Foundation: "Our own response of love allows God's life to flow into us without limit." Our response to this longing is one of love when we acknowledge that it is happening and we pause to see what God might be inviting us to tend to.

How do we respond with love to God? What do your responses look like? Are they visible to the outside world? Are they intimate words and actions between you and God?

What do you think God is inviting you to at this time in your life?

God's Living Water

God is longing for us. Longing to be in relationship with us. To offer us the very intimacy we seek even with our dark parts, our sin, aspects of our lives that are not all in order. God longs to be in relationship with us because God created us and loves us. Not only does God long to be in relationship with us, but God also longs to offer us the living water that Jesus offered the woman at the well. The living waters of love, mercy, and forgiveness. Living waters that console us, heal us, strengthen us, lift us up, unbind us, and set us free. God longs to bring us along a path that offers peace the world cannot give.

How is the love God longs to bring us different from the peace offered by the world?

How do you feel about the notion of experiencing intimacy with God? What makes a relationship intimate?

An Invitation

Getting to know Jesus changed my life. My relationship with Jesus still changes me as I am drawn ever deeper into the waters of intimacy with him. The Good News I so desperately and urgently want to share with each of you is that this relationship is available to you. Not only is it available, but Jesus is already inviting you into it. Jesus is standing on the shore next to us long before we realize it, inviting us into the waters of relationship with him.

In what ways (big or small) has knowing Jesus changed your life?

What can you do to get to know Jesus better, to deepen your relationship with him? Are you willing to do whatever it takes to make this happen?

Interior Knowing

Jesus calls each of us into relationship, just as he called the first disciples. His invitation to them was, "Follow me, and I will make you fish for people." They dropped their nets and followed him (Matthew 4:18–22; Mark 1:16–20; Luke 5:11). As they began their relationship with Jesus and walked with him, they learned who he was, how he loved, and how to follow him in their daily lives. The same is true for each of us. We are invited to get to know Jesus intimately so, as stated in the Spiritual Exercises of St. Ignatius, we can have "interior knowledge of the Lord . . . so that we might love Him and follow Him more closely" (SE 104).

What does it mean to have interior knowledge of the Lord?

Is there someone in your life with whom you share this type of intimate friendship?

Initial Encounter

What was your initial encounter with Jesus? Maybe you are in the middle of an initial net-dropping moment right now. Maybe your call to enter a relationship with Jesus came years ago. Maybe there is a deeper invitation from Jesus to drop everything and follow him even more closely. The invitation continues throughout our lives to embrace the gift of friendship with Jesus and to get to know him in a tangible, personal way. The promises of God help us to open up and become free to follow Jesus. We are invited to come and see, to follow Jesus, and to leave our nets behind. As we do, our lives will transform.

What would you identify as your initial encounter or net-dropping moment with Jesus?

When has this invitation reoccurred in your life? What was your response?

A Call

A grace we are suggested to pray for in the Spiritual Exercises of St. Ignatius is for God to help us get to know Jesus more intimately, to love him more intensely, and to follow Jesus more closely. Ultimately, what this means is becoming more like Jesus by learning to see like Jesus, hear like Jesus, love like Jesus, and act like Jesus. It means not only hearing the call to follow Jesus but also to walk with him and be there working with him. As we get to know him and to love him, we learn to follow his way and live the model he lays out for us.

Is there someone you know who goes through life seeing, hearing, loving, and acting in Christlike ways? Can you borrow from their example and apply it to your life?

How do you strive to do this in your life? Would your actions inspire someone else to imitate Jesus?

Healing Power

Contemplating the way Jesus healed people has a profound impact on me. As I watch Jesus heal people such as the man with the withered hand, the hemorrhaging woman, the paralyzed man on the mat, the crippled woman, and so many more, it reminds me that the same power available to them to be healed is available to us. It is through our connection with Jesus—our time with him in the inner chapel—that his power moves from him to us. When we go to our inner chapel, we encounter Jesus the same way Jesus encountered people tangibly when he was walking around on earth.

When was a time you felt Jesus's power move from him to you?

How might we meet Jesus in the same way that he met others when he walked the earth?

Personal Encounters

So, imagine each day encountering Jesus in a personal way in your inner chapel—over and over again receiving the gift of his love, his mercy, and his friendship. This is how we are transformed—by going to our inner chapels every day and letting the healing power of Jesus into our hearts. Eventually, that power permeates our lives and is passed along to those who need it.

What might help your encounters with Jesus be more personal?

What are the things that might be preventing the power of Jesus from spreading all throughout your life?

Overflowing Love

When we are making progress in the spiritual life, Ignatius says that the Holy Spirit feels like a drop of water that gently soaks into a sponge versus the evil spirit feeling like water hitting a stone. I believe encountering Jesus in our inner chapel feels like gentle drops of water soaking into a sponge. Over time, as we continue to encounter Jesus, the drops of water saturate the sponge to the point that the sponge can no longer hold the water anymore. The water begins oozing out of the sponge to the surfaces around it. This is how it is with us. Our relationship with Jesus is never just about us; it is about understanding who he is in an experiential, interior way so that we can bring the gifts of this relationship out into the world.

Who in your life has gifted you with an overflowing abundance of love? What did you do with that gift?

How is this dynamic of receiving-sharing relevant to a meaningful relationship with Jesus?

God's Promise of Renewal

Weariness comes in all shapes and sizes. Sometimes it comes from burning the candle at both ends. Other times it stems from carrying a heavy load for a long time. Weariness comes from holding on to a job, a relationship, or even a call from God long after we were invited to let it go. It can hit us after an intense season that required more effort and a more rapid pace than are normal for us. The weight of our tiredness can overwhelm and surprise us when we finally notice it. The exhaustion can go far beyond just the physical and can also become weariness of mind and spirit. Thank goodness God promises us rest! Going to the inner chapel provides rest.

Reflect on a time in your life when you experienced fatigue so complete, it seemed to envelop you from the outside all the way into your soul.

What precipitated this feeling? How did God bring you rest?

Consolation and Feeling Alive

St. Ignatius offers many tools from his discernment wisdom to help us notice our thirst for rest. Much of his discernment wisdom is about noticing the movements of consolation and desolation in our lives. Consolation is an experience of feeling on fire with God's love that impels us to love and serve God and love and serve others. Consolation often inspires gratitude toward God for all God's gifts of love, mercy, friendship, and faithfulness. When we are in consolation, we might feel more alive, more connected to God and to other people.

What do you do, or what can you do when you need solace, comfort, rest?

Reflect on a time in your life when you felt both more alive and more connected to God and to other people. What can you do to receive this gift of consolation from God?

Understanding Desolation

While in consolation we feel increases in hope, faith, love, and a rise in energy for love and service to God and others, in desolation we feel the exact opposite. We might feel a tiredness or heaviness. We might feel disconnected from God and from people. Our energy and passion decrease. St. Ignatius suggests that when we notice signs of desolation, we need to pause and dig into them and notice what the cause might be.

What have been some of the moments of desolation in your life?

What helps you feel more closely connected with God?

The Impact of Rest

When we leave rest unattended, it impacts all areas of our life, including our bodies. We struggle to sleep, to fall asleep, and to stay asleep. Weariness raises blood pressure and causes inflammation. It can trigger unhealthy changes in diet because we tend to reach for sugar and caffeine when our energy is low. Weariness, whether of body or spirit, will weaken the immune system and dull our reactions, making us vulnerable to illness and injury.

What are you doing to help, and what are you doing to hinder, your rest and sleep?

If you are experiencing weariness, what might be at the root of it?

Coming to Jesus

The Good News for us is that we are not completely on our own when it comes to rest. God supports us and helps us by providing invitations for rest and by helping us refresh ourselves and recover our strength. Where do we go for rest, and how can we embrace this promise of God's rest for the weary? In the Gospel of Matthew, Jesus says, "Come to me, all you that are weary and are carrying heavy burdens, and I will give you rest" (Matthew 11:28). Jesus tells us that if we come to him, he will give us rest and lighten our loads. Our part is to come to him, and Jesus, who is our still point, is the source of our rest.

When, where, and how do you bring yourself to Jesus in response to his invitation?

In the past, how has Jesus lightened your load or provided you solace and a safe place to rest?

Be Still and Know

One of my favorite coffee mugs to use each morning is the one my friend Ann gave me when my first book was published. It is a beautiful white ceramic mug with a gold handle, and in beautiful gold letters are the words *Be still and know.* These four words are from Psalm 46:10: "Be still, and know that I am God." Often in the quiet of the mornings as I hold this mug in my hands, feel its warmth, and breathe deeply in the quiet, I am overwhelmed with gratitude that someone taught me that the inner chapel existed in the first place. As I still my body, embrace the silence, and go to my inner chapel, I lean in to the source of my rest and also the source of my daily strength. This daily stopping to be still and to know that God is there continues to transform my life.

How hard or easy is it for you to be still? What helps you to find stillness?

How can knowing that God is here with us transform our lives?

Surrendering Control

Sometimes, we resist allowing God to be part of our process because it means giving up control and surrendering. It makes us feel good and safe when we feel we are in control or when we have all the pieces and parts in our hands. It can make us feel good about ourselves that we can do something on our own. In so many ways, when we don't allow God to help carry our burden, pride rules the day. Pride to me is ultimately saying, "I trust myself more than you, God." Let me tell you from experience that it's much easier to let God into situations, to stand shoulder to shoulder with Jesus, and to not go it alone. Letting go is not an easy thing to do, but when we do, we give God room to come in the most unexpected ways and offer rest, strength, and nourishment.

Do you find it easy or hard to give up control? To surrender? Why or why not?

Why is it prideful to not relinquish control to God or to refrain from asking God to help us shoulder our burdens?

Showing Up Honestly

Rest comes to us in prayer in all kinds of ways. God who sees us gives us what we need even when we do not know we need it. God pours into us the theological virtues of faith, hope, and love. These three have their source in God alone. We cannot have faith without God. We do not love without God. We do not hope without God. All it takes is for us to show up in the inner chapel with honesty and share with God what we long for. God opens us to receive the theological virtues, also fruits of the Holy Spirit.

What does it take to show up in the inner chapel with honesty?

What is it that you are longing for at this moment in your life?

Renewing the Dry Land

Close your eyes and go to your inner chapel. Imagine that you and Jesus are surveying your life together, noticing the places in your life that are "sun-scorched"—dry and arid. Together, you notice all the places that are in need of water. Imagine you and Jesus walking up to each parched area of your life. Talk to Jesus about what you see. Listen to what he tells you about this area of your life. Then, watch as Jesus pours his living water into this sun-scorched area of your life.

What part(s) of your life is (are) sun-scorched?

How does Jesus's gift of living water satisfy your thirst? How does it renew and restore the parched land?

Stillness in Change

Even though life changes, there is a constant other than change. Throughout the centuries, there is a steady, unshakable, consistent, enduring presence in our world: God. Through the ages and all human development, God remains. Throughout our salvation story, we can see God's consistency and steadiness in human experience. Human beings have changed in their understanding of God, but God has always remained.

How does the unchanging nature of God comfort and assist you amid upheaval and change?

What can you do to become more aware of God's steady presence as you go through your day?

Intimacy with God

Scripture shows us God's desire for relationship with us. Never wanting only a superficial relationship, God sought intimacy with us. God seeks intimacy with us now. We are not different from the people in the Scriptures. We are women at the well harboring secrets that God already knows and we yearn to share. We are blind men yearning for sight. We are the lost son hoping that our absence will be noticed. We are Naomi and Ruth clinging to each other after mourning multiple deaths. We are Sarah without a child. In each of these situations, God encounters people and offers them the gift of relationship and spiritual intimacy. God offers this gift to us, too.

What person(s) from Scripture do you relate to when it comes to your relationship with God?

What constitutes intimacy in a relationship, and how can this aspect of relationships be cultivated in your relationship with God?

Deep Connections

I believe that we all want to be loved, to be familiar to someone, and to have our stories and lives known in a deep way by another person. The most utter despair and hopelessness that I witness in people is when they are going through life without an intimate relationship with another person. This loneliness, disconnection, and isolation at times can pull us to a dark place.

Who are the people in your life who "know your story" in a deep way? With whom do you long to share your story in a deeper way?

How can you share your story with God?

Steadfast Love

This is the promise of God that Psalm 136 so passionately proclaims repeatedly: "His steadfast love endures forever." God offers us the invitation to open ourselves to God's love, to embrace the gift of God's love, and to accept that we cannot be separated from God. This is truly the gift of God's mercy. God will never stop initiating and attempting to draw us into a relationship. God will continue to woo and pursue us.

Think of an example from your life when you were dating someone. Reflect on the experience.

What does it mean to you to know that God will always continue to woo and pursue you?

True Identity

In our spiritual intimacy with God, we grow to understand that our identity is inseparable from our relationship with God. Our key, defining relationships with other people will change eventually, but our relationship with God is the core of who we are. Our identity doesn't come from what we do, what role we play, where we live, or what we own, but simply from the person we are in God. This is true for each of us. This offer of the source of our identity is not found through our tasks, our goals, our ambitions, our relationships, or anything else, but in the fact that we are inseparable from God and therefore never alone.

Why is our relationship with God so crucial to knowing our true identity?

How does knowing God help us to know ourselves?

Soul Reflections

Go to your inner chapel. As you settle into this special place of strength, shelter, and refuge, invite God to help you recall a time when you struggled to believe God saw you or was with you as you experienced it. As you reflect on it, ask God to show you ways that God saw you, sheltered you, and offered you what you needed to face the next thing.

When have you struggled to believe that God sees you and is with you?

To whom might you turn, and what might you do, when you are feeling this way?

God in Loneliness

Embracing God's gift of the inner chapel helps me tremendously when I experience loneliness. By visiting it each day for almost two decades, I believe I am finally beginning to understand the words in the Gospel of John where Jesus promises us the Advocate—the Holy Spirit—and promises us we will never be alone: "I will not leave you orphaned" (John 14:18). When I think of these words and repeat them to myself, something inside shifts and brings a bit of light into the dark loneliness. Remembering that God promises to be with me and that I am never alone is deeply comforting. When I first began to understand this years ago, it caused a life-altering shift, one I am still trying to deepen and believe in more.

In what situations do you find yourself experiencing loneliness?

Who helps you recalibrate your thoughts so that you again realize that God is with you and that you are never alone?

Emmanuel

Because each of us has an inner chapel, we can meet God there at any time. This is true regardless of where we are, what we're doing, what we are facing, or what is happening around us. We believe in the Incarnation: God became flesh and made his dwelling among us. Emmanuel means "God with us."

How is belief in the Incarnation important to one's prayer life?

When or how have you most experienced Emmanuel ("God with us") in your life?

Belonging to God

There is deep comfort in knowing that I belong to God, that I am known by God, and that I know God. Even when relationships change around me, I still belong to God. When life shifts and my communities change, one thing always remains: I belong to Someone who knows me and loves me deeply.

How does God let you know that you belong to him?

What are some of the ways that you have experienced profound changes and shifts in your life? How has God brought you comfort during those times?

Unique Creations

We belong to God because we were created and formed by God. Our very existence comes out of a creative act of love by God who cared deeply enough about us to form us in a unique, unrepeatable way. There is no one, not one other person in this world, who is like you or me. We belong to God, our creator.

What unique qualities did God instill in you that you believe God delights in?

How do you use these qualities to touch the lives of others?

Named and Claimed

We are named and claimed by God. Yes, we are given our names by our parents and those who raise us, but we are also named and claimed by God in our relationship with God. Many times, the Scriptures proclaim, "You will be my people, and I will be your God."

What does it mean to you to know that you are named and claimed by God?

How does it feel in a world full of change to know you always belong to God?

Chosen and Called

We are chosen and called. God chose us to be in relationship with God. God chooses us as God's people. God calls us not only into relationship with God but also to use our gifts and calls in a unique way. On days when I am close to forgetting this promise, I repeat these words like a mantra: I am created and formed, named and claimed, chosen and called.

Reflect on a moment in your life when you felt chosen by God. How did God help you know you were called to be in intimate relationship with God?

Whom do you believe God has chosen you to be, and what do you think God has chosen you to do?

Jesus's Humanity

It's easy to think that Jesus popped out of Mary's womb understanding all the mysteries of the world, including the fact that he was fully loved by God. If we think like this, though, we underestimate the fact that Jesus was human—fully human. Jesus entered humanity so that we can understand the way to live fully loved. This means that Jesus grew into his understanding of God's love for him just as we do.

What stories from the Gospels most remind you of the full humanity of Jesus?

How does this awareness of Jesus's humanity help you grow in your understanding and appreciation of God's love for you?

Gestures of Holiness

Looking back over our life stories, can we name people who showed us that we have value or worth because of the concrete gestures of holiness they offered us? Meals provided by a parent or family member; a loved one providing shelter for us when we were growing up; a teacher investing a little extra time to help us understand a topic; a coach or extracurricular teacher seeing a talent in us and having the courage to push us to use it to its fullest; a significant other caring to hear about our day; a friend showing up to celebrate a moment or be present during a difficult time. When I look back over my life, I can name many ways that I came to understand God's love for me through the concrete gestures of others.

Who are the people in your life who offered you concrete gestures of holiness that help you recognize God's love for you? Who helps you be confident in your value and worth?

Toward whom are you called to demonstrate similar gestures of holiness?

Moments of God's Love

Wouldn't it be amazing if the sky opened and a dove descended over our heads and God spoke words aloud to us? My guess is that this hasn't happened. However, I bet we can name events or moments that have opened our capacity to accept God's love for us. Moments that provided a brief glimpse of us as people loved just as we are.

Recall and reflect on moments in your life that opened your capacity to accept God's love.

How have you helped others to recognize that they are loved?

Desiring to Step

Our desire to be loved fully and wholeheartedly by God is one of the ways the Holy Spirit works within us. As Pope Francis reminds us, all we need is to desire to take the step: "The medicine is there, the healing is there—if only we take a small step toward God . . . or even just desire to take that step." God will meet us in this desire to be loved and will increase that desire.

How does one take a step toward God?

How can even just the desire to be near to God draw us to the healing grace of the Holy Spirit?

The Unconditional

Our ability to reason can get in the way of receiving God's love because we can rationalize and list all the ways we are not worthy of God's love (or maybe we feel another person is not worthy of this freely given gift). Fortunately, God doesn't operate by our standards. We are loved as we are right now. Our task on this journey of faith is to increase our capacity to receive God's gift of love.

How can reason get in the way of receiving God's love?

In what ways are we blessed and fortunate that God's love is not based on logic?

Overcoming the Voices

We sometimes get in our own way when it comes to accepting God's love for us. We listen to other voices that tell us we are not worthy to receive God's love. Voices speaking words such as: you have to earn your worth; you have to get to a certain point on your faith journey before you are loved; your worthiness of love is measured by what you own, what you do, or the amount of money you make; you are not qualified.

What are some of the other voices that you consider to be most prevalent in today's world?

How do these voices interfere with our ability to accept God's love for us?

Openness and Resistance

It is important for us to look at where we opened to God's love and also where we might feel closed to receiving God's love because God continues to create us moment by moment. God is loving us through the movements of openness and resistance. God loves us through the moments we are proud of and the ones we are ashamed of. God loves us through the moments we overcome temptation and the ones we succumb to temptation. God loves us in all the moments that remind us we are lovable and those moments that make us feel unlovable. God is always with us, loving us, tending to us moment by moment. We are never a finished product but an ongoing creation that the Creator continues to shape and mold.

Why do you think we sometimes resist God's love?

In what ways is the Creator shaping and molding you at this point in your life?

Transforming Love

What I know from my own life and from witnessing others grow in their relationship with God through spiritual direction is that something profound happens when a person opens to the unconditional love of God. I am convinced that we will never fully understand the magnitude of God's love, but I think much of our faith journey is trying to open ourselves, every day, a little bit more, to God's transforming love.

Why is unconditional love so transforming?

How have you opened yourself to the unconditional love of God?

Listening to God

I've spent much of my adult life seeking to free myself from the voices of other people and to listen more fully to God's voice. In so many ways, I lived like the woman crippled for eighteen years that we read about in Luke's Gospel. As it says, she had a "spirit that had crippled her for eighteen years. She was bent over and was quite unable to stand up straight" (Luke 13:11). While I was not physically bent over by a spirit, listening to other people's voices over God's was weighing me down, keeping me completely incapable of standing erect.

What are some messages in your life that have weighed you down?

What helps us hear God through the clamor of other people's voices?

The Gift of Infinite Mercy

Sometimes our own voice gets in the way of our believing in God's promise of infinite mercy. We sometimes believe that our story is already finished and we can't change it. We are left feeling stuck, paralyzed, bound, and helpless. But wherever we are now, God meets us there—and does not leave us there! God is going to do everything—and I mean everything—to set us free from what inhibits us, stops us, and leaves us unfree. God protects against and counteracts our human actions and then offers to us new space and life. God offers us mercy.

When was a time that your own voice got in the way of believing in God's promise of infinite mercy?

What can you do to free yourself from those doubts when they undermine your confidence in God's promise?

All Things New

Mercy means God's refusal to leave us where we are. God will not leave us broken, bruised, exhausted, and tired without any hope for new life or new possibilities. God's mercy means always seeking to make all things new. Jesus promised, "I will not leave you orphaned" (John 14:18). Jesus is with us in all we are facing. Jesus sees what we see; he also entered the world and experienced it as a human. As he entered the world, he brought inextinguishable light.

Reflect on a time when you witnessed someone act with mercy by refusing to leave someone who was broken, bruised, exhausted, tired, and without hope.

Reflect on a time when God's mercy made all things new for you.

In Need of Mercy

Jesus's mission was to the poor, the captive, the blind, the oppressed, the brokenhearted, the mourning. Jesus's promise of mercy is for each of us right now. We are the ones physically and spiritually poor who need a Savior. We are the ones held captive by sin. We are the ones burdened. We are the ones aching with brokenness. We are the ones grieving and mourning. We are the ones in need of mercy. We are the ones seeking to be made well.

In what area of your life do you most need to experience God's mercy?

How can you bring God's mercy to someone else in need of a Savior?

More than Moments

It does not matter what we have: possessions, past experiences, education, or work experiences. It does not matter what we do: for a living, with our life, with our choices. It does not matter what people say about us: whether it is the best compliment or the worst insult. Jesus reminds us that we are more to him than the worst thing we've ever done and even more than the best moment of our lives. Our identity is wrapped up in the mere fact that we are fully seen just as we are and loved unconditionally anyway.

Think of some of the finest accomplishments and, conversely, the greatest failures of your life. What does it mean to you that you are more to God than these moments?

Who in your life needs to hear and embrace this message?

Reflecting on Sin

In the first week of the Spiritual Exercises, we are invited to reflect on our personal experience of sin and comprehend sin not with our heads but with our hearts. We are invited to see sin as God sees it within the context of God's love. Ignatius invites us to take a hard look at our lives and the realities of sin, but not before we have a full understanding of God's unconditional love for us. Before we face our sin, we need to understand that who we are is not rooted in what we have done or not done but in simply being loved by God.

Why is it so important to face sin within the context of God's unconditional love for us?

How do we reflect on and comprehend our personal experiences of sin, not with our heads but with our hearts?

False Idols

Sin is a disruption of God's plans for us. Sometimes it happens when we turn away from God, but most often it occurs when we run after false idols, and when we do this, we unravel God's hopes and plans for us. St. Ignatius calls these disordered attachments. Disordered attachments can be our desires, our limited hopes, our possessions, our plans, our relationships, or our ambitions. Ultimately, they are people, desires, or things that we become more attached to than we are to God.

What are some of the false idols that grab the attention of people today?

What disordered attachment(s) in your life could be disrupting God's plans for you?

Liberty

Our awareness of this capacity to sin leads us right into our need for a Savior. Being aware of our sinfulness is part of accepting our own poverty, that we are utterly dependent on God to overcome our sin and receive mercy. God's mercy frees us, and it also helps us become aware of our sinful tendencies. God gives us sight to see ourselves as God sees us. We learn to see our worth and belovedness but also whatever gets in the way of our receiving God's love and mercy.

How is being utterly dependent on a Savior to overcome our sinfulness liberating?

What sinfulness in your life might God be calling you to see more honestly? How can God's mercy liberate you from this poverty?

The Gift of Unease

One of the ways the Holy Spirit helps us is to show us when we have made a choice or a decision that does not lead us closer to God. Often the support of the Holy Spirit comes through a feeling even more than actual sight. We feel the support of the Holy Spirit awakening us to our sinfulness through restlessness that often feels like remorse or the sting of conscience. When our restlessness is due to a choice we have made that is not in alignment with who we are in God, we might notice feelings of guilt, disquiet, remorse, regret, or sorrow. While these feelings are uncomfortable, they can be gifts of the Holy Spirit that help us wake up to something we've done or said that inhibits our growth in God.

When was a time in your life that the Holy Spirit helped you revisit a choice that was not leading you closer to God?

How can restlessness or disquiet be a gift of the Holy Spirit?

A Soothing Balm

No matter what we name as our brokenness, God sees it and seeks to enter it and to heal it. God wants to pour the soothing balm of mercy upon what binds us, what has deeply hurt us, and what burdens us. The need for healing might be grief of loss, broken relationship, betrayal, or abandonment. Healing also must occur where our own sinfulness has caused harm.

What would you name as your brokenness?

Into what area(s) of your life do you most need God to pour the soothing balm of mercy?

Three-Way Call

St. Ignatius offers a beautiful prayer tool called the triple colloquy. Colloquy simply means conversation. He invites us to take the sorrow we feel over our brokenness, the sin we have named in ourselves, or the sin we see in the world into our prayer. As we carry the areas of our lives and the world that are in need of God's mercy to prayer, we pause and have three intimate conversations: first with Mary, then with Jesus, and then with God. At the end of each conversation we ask, What have I done for Christ? What am I doing for Christ? What ought I do for Christ?

How would you answer the three questions posed above about an area of your life that needs God's mercy?

Do you see the infinite possibilities for helping others by employing this strategy for having thoughtful conversations with others?

A Companion in Suffering

We all encounter suffering, either our own or someone else's. Perhaps our suffering or the suffering we witness is not like Jesus's agony on the cross or like my grandfather's cancer journey, but in our own way we experience and witness hurt, abandonment, betrayal, loss, doubt, fear, or pain. It is hard to endure suffering and also watch another person suffer. If it is our own suffering we are facing, we tend to yearn for someone to stay with us, be present to us, and listen to us. If we are faced with another's suffering, we may be invited to stay with the other person, to be present, even when no words can be offered. No matter which role we play, we can rest assured that Jesus is our companion in it. Jesus who was entirely human experienced the full range of humanity, good and bad.

Who has been present to you when you were suffering? What did their presence mean to you, and what was its effect on you? Is there someone for whom you have been present during their time of need?

How has Jesus been present to you in times of suffering?

The Richness of Spiritual Poverty

Spiritual poverty is utter reliance on God. We encounter spiritual poverty in those moments when no amount of money or power or influence or medicine or anything else can change the reality of the circumstances. I think we feel invincible at times as human beings, thinking that we can control all situations due to our intelligence, finances, relationships, or power. From my experience and from listening to others describe their experiences, I believe that at some point every person is stripped of everything and faced with the truth that we utterly depend on God.

When was a time that you felt stripped of everything and yet were aware that you were utterly dependent on God?

What feelings does this realization bring about in you? How is this insight both frightening and healing?

New Life

New life does come. One sign of new life that comes after suffering is that we become more loving, more faithful, more generous, and more compassionate. St. Ignatius says, "There are truths that can be discovered only through suffering or from the critical vantage point of extreme situations." I can honestly say that there are truths I learned through suffering that, while I do not want to go through such pain again, I consider great gifts of understanding, for which I am grateful.

What truths have you learned through suffering?

Reflect on a time when you experienced new life after an experience of suffering. What did God teach you?

Moment by Moment

God creates us moment by moment. We are not stagnant, frozen-in-time beings. We are malleable, ongoing works of God's creation. While God's instruments of creation in nature are wind, fire, and water, God uses our gifts, our circumstances, our prayer lives, and our experiences to continue creating us, moment after moment. God labors on our behalf long before we realize it. God was part of our conception and birth, making us the unique human beings we are—down to our sex, race, hair color, eye color, and personality traits. We had no control over the family we were born into and the city where we were born. God continues creating us moment by moment.

In what ways do you experience God creating you moment by moment?

What helps you to be more open to God's continuing creation of you?

Unique Callings

What we find in looking back is that throughout the ongoing creation, there are common threads that tie our unique callings to the work of spreading the Good News. There is not another human being on this planet who looks the same as you do or I do or who has the same experiences and relationships. As we notice and name God's gift of ongoing creation, we can offer to God all our gifts, experiences, and understandings.

As you look back over God's ongoing creation of you, what are some of the most significant experiences that have shaped you?

What gifts do you possess that you can offer to God?

Courageous Faith

So often we think that these calls are set aside for special people like our saints and not for each of us in our ordinary lives. This could not be further from the truth. The saints serve as our great cloud of witnesses, giving us examples of how to live courageous and bold lives of faith. They are not to be examples of holiness that make us feel that we cannot obtain what they did. Each of us has the promise of being personally invited by Jesus into a relationship and being uniquely chosen and called into service to God according to our gifts.

When it comes to the saints, who among the great cloud of witnesses stands out?

Do you know people who are living their faith courageously and boldly?

Yes!

If our restlessness is stemming from our no when God is clearly inviting us to say yes, then the disquiet within us will subside when we say yes. Maybe God is birthing a new call within us, and while we notice the nudge toward a new yes, we are saying no with our words and our actions. The gift of the restlessness is helping us know that God steps forward for us. Restlessness often calms when we step forward in faith and say yes to what God is asking of us.

When was a time that you struggled to say yes to God?

In what ways does God nudge you toward a new yes?

Pay Attention

Notice what you are noticing. That is one of my favorite lines, and I say it often in spiritual direction. I feel that discernment is about noticing. Noticing the promises of God at work in our life. Noticing the love given to us by God. Noticing the deep desires in our hearts to respond to the love given to us. Noticing the longings of other people. Noticing our gifts. Noticing the way God is inviting us to respond to the longings we see with the gifts we are given. Noticing the movements of the Holy Spirit. It is all about noticing.

In your moments of quiet and stillness, what are you noticing?

What helps you to notice more deeply the movements of God in your life?

The Nearness of Jesus

Jesus is still with each one of us today. That's the hope of the Resurrection. We have so many reasons to rejoice. We can rejoice in Jesus's presence in our lives and in the generous promises he continues to abundantly share with us. In Philippians it says, "Rejoice the Lord is near." The Lord is near to every one of us. He is so near that he abides in our inner chapels and is inseparable from us. This is why we can hope. The Lord is near.

How do you notice the nearness of Jesus in your life?

What are the reasons you can rejoice in the hope of the Lord?

Sharing the Gift

May you come to understand in a bone-deep knowing way what the lived reality of the promises of God can do in our life. May you go to your inner chapel and meet God there and discover the gifts and promises that await you. May the love we receive from God turn into actions that invite others to know the promises and share them with others.

Who in your life needs to know the inner chapel exists? Who needs to hear the promises of God?

How might you share this gift with those people?

About the Author

Becky Eldredge is an Ignatian-trained spiritual director, retreat facilitator, and writer who is passionate about helping people live and lead with Christ. She is the founder of Ignatian Ministries, a nonprofit ministry that supports people seeking a deeper relationship with Christ by offering retreats, prayer and discernment resources, and community.

Becky accompanies clergy, religious, and lay leaders through the Spiritual Exercises of St. Ignatius, retreats, spiritual direction, and various professional development programs focused on the interior life. She is part of the teaching staff at the Archdiocese of New Orleans Spirituality Center, where she trains spiritual directors in the Ignatian tradition.

Becky is the author of two award-winning books, *The Inner Chapel* and *Busy Lives & Restless Souls*. She lives in Baton Rouge, Louisiana, with her husband Chris and their three children, Brady, Abby, and Mary.